Spirit comes to EARTH

Renewing Your Heart's Mission

for people from 11 to 101

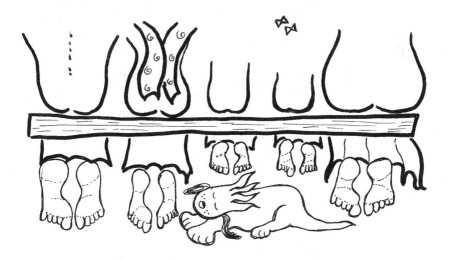

Poems and Art of *Eleven*

Peace
Love
Karma

Peace Love Karma Publishing, 607 Elmira Rd. #266, Vacaville, CA. 95687
Visit our website at http://www.peacelovekarma.com or order toll free 1-866-888-7272
Manufactured and printed in the U.S.A.

Publisher's Cataloging-in-Publication
(*Provided by Quality Books, Inc.*)

   Eleven.
      Spirit comes to earth : renewing your heart's mission -- for people from 11 to 101 /
   poems and art by Eleven. -- 1st ed.
      p. cm.
      Includes bibliographical references and index.
      LCCN 2003109779
      ISBN 0-9743540-0-7 (perfect bound)
      ISBN 0-9743540-2-3 (Hardcover Lib. bind)

      1. Environmentalism--Poetry 2. Self-actualization
   (Psychology)--Poetry. 3. Spiritual life--Christianity--
   Poetry. I. Title

   PS3605.L384S65 2004   811'.6
                       QBI33-2024

         First Edition May 2005
          9 8 7 6 5 4 3 2 1

Dedication

To My Family and friends,
New and old, Earthbound and in Spirit...
May the Great Spirit bring more abundance
to you than you are willing or able to receive.

To God,
the one who created everything on Earth.
"Oh Lord our God,
all this store that we have prepared ...For thine holy
name cometh of thy hand and is all thine own."

1 Chronicles 29:16

To Mother Earth,
May God Bless our ship of the Universe.

And To My daughter, Celena and My Mother, Joan
who brought me great love down from heaven above,
With love always.

"And to many, I am just as free...
As you are here, I am here also.
Try as you might, never can you, be me...
Inside each haven, the safeguard of time."

Introduction

I believe connecting to your spiritual purpose is the most important thing you will ever aspire to do on this planet. Everyone needs to feel this connection to his or her higher source when living, working, resting and playing. This connection will guide you to find and live your true gifts that will allow incredible happiness and love into your daily life. You certainly deserve to feel loved and to be happy.

How do you find your spiritual gift? First, you discover what creative activity truly makes you feel whole and joyful. *This is* your naturally given "gift" from Spirit. This pathway for contentment flows easily to you. Second, you consciously live connected to your higher source, your God and your Spirit or whatever you may call the universal creator. You learn to listen to your "Spirit" and "hear" the messages you are given. Your life will change dramatically when you listen and learn, listen and do, listen and trust your "Spirit" to be your best friend.

Imagine this…you have a special reason and a true gift that you were born to accomplish in this life. YOU are the only one on this planet that can do or see, or be, or learn, or channel your special information or art, or knowledge to Earth. ONLY YOU! You must find this gift by remembering your Spirit, and then you will lead a truly happy and fulfilled life with great purpose for all your Earth days. Your new life will begin the very moment you decide to serve the reason you came to Earth. Imagine if just HALF of the people on Earth had found and were living their purpose in life. The Earth would experience many gifts and much advancement. What a different world we would live in!

Seek your spiritual connection within your realm of purpose and strengthen all aspects of your life. Every soul who lives an Earth Life seeks to create wholeness in their heart and on this planet. Your connection to "the Whole" is a definite part of your human and spiritual experience. Sharing your gift is required! Your Spirit Family will grant you great happiness, health and wealth in return. YOU ARE GIFTED and have a special need to fulfill, thought to communicate and unique beauty to share. Your gift from Spirit is not dependent on your sex, age, religion or the country where you live. JUST LISTEN! Trust your heart and the Spirit of light will guide you to find contentment.

Everyone has a dream... are you fulfilling yours? Everyone has a voice - are you singing or silent? Everybody has a song in his or her heart to sing; a book in his or her lifetime to write; a garden in his or her community to plant and a family or friends to love, nurture and assist. Turn your life and Spirit ON by focusing on sharing your gift. Spend your days delivering a gift that comes directly from your heart, thus nurturing your very soul. You will feel alive and time will fly!

My wish for you is to live your gift today. Begin early in life if you can, around school and work assignments but start when you realize where your love lies and make a choice to "bring it down to Earth" for all to enjoy. Seek happiness with all your heart and Spirit. Long or short, you will live an abundant life by "being" your "gift". Find your unique purpose in living and help us preserve the Earth for our children.

I invite you to become an Earth Advocate. Help us to make Earth a sustainable environment for future generations. Our struggling Earth needs our attention and love to continue her journey and to assist us in continuing our journey. Let us commit to our Earth and our Spirit and find our paradise on Earth on a personal and planetary level.

I invite you to join our Spirit Family. Begin your journey today and seek these treasure chests of the Stationary mind that only YOU can unlock. I hope your "Spirit comes to Earth" and all your dreams are fulfilled. May your Spirit and our Planet are healed by your loving gifts.

Sincerely,

Eleven

Your Spiritual and Earth Advocate

SPIRIT comes to EARTH

Paradise on Earth

You should go about
selecting additions to your spiritual life
with the same attention as you go about selecting
clothing, cars or gifts.

To make real progress spiritually,
we must feed our Spirits properly
with foods called inspiration,
love and kindness.

Your Spirit, like your mind and body
requires replenishing on a daily basis.

Vitamins
like prayer, faith and meditation.
Conditioners
like freedom of thought and full self-expression.
Lotions
like poetry, music, encouragement and understanding.

Your Spirit, that part of you that God
enhances with his very being,
needs to be remembered in this life
as your true self.
Not your physical body!

It is mind's punishment that it has lost
the eye to see each human's true Spirit.
Spirit fell from grace and only radiates dimly
within the body of most,
and your mind must be opened to see once again….
but you know what I say to be true! Will you remember?

You should go about selecting additions
to your spiritual being,

as earnestly and skillfully as you can.
Prepare like a student selecting a college.
Trust and follow like a child learning to walk.

Your Spirit may lack only as long as you neglect it
as a ghost that has never existed.
Plan to know yourself as well
as you know your favorite hobby.

Fill your storehouse as a family would
who must keep well supplied through a long winter snow.
Seek your dreams with such urgency,
as though you will surely die tomorrow
and your time may not be enough to complete your tasks.

When you feel Spirit's friendly pull on your heart
in sorrow,
its incredible heights of good vibration in your laughter or
in the hymns that rise up and sing out of your heart, act!

Like a child who needs a teacher say,
"Yes, yes my Spirit.
I acknowledge you.
I see you are hungry and I will feed you.
I see you are present and I will not forsake you.
I know you are my very essence and
I seek to know you, love you and
forgive you.
You are my pathway to heaven and God.
You are my gift that I shall not squander.
You are my rainbow in this world of rain."

Believe me when I say,
I want to know myself, my Spirit.

I will find time to feed these daily hungers and cravings
of my Spirit by exercising my body and my mind,
by filling my store house with spiritual fruits,
by following my dreams,
by showing loving kindness towards humans,
by slowing down my race
through material land,
and by looking inside my heart more often
so I know myself completely.

I am responsible for my spiritual growth, therefore
I will sing more often.
I will pray and meditate in silence more often.
I will dream and let my body not keep me in slumber.
I will eat more fresh vegetables and fruits
to strengthen my mind and body.
I will drink from the cup of satisfaction,
and promise to not forget the part of myself
that no one can contribute to but me.

My Spirit! I will learn to like myself.
I forgive others and myself, for my errors.
I wipe the slate clean of all past hurt.
I begin today!

My Spirit! Let it sing praises to this life
as silently as the dew falls.

Let me spread love and happiness to others
with nothing expected in return.

Let me shine so brightly through my skin
that my Spirit touches everyone I meet.

Let me know my true self and my purpose and
I will have found true paradise on Earth.

Spiritual Attraction

A Spirit should attract to itself
the highest vibration possible.
Staying in the same surroundings
with the same materials and objects around you,
molds those material vibrations to you.

The highest vibration is God, the Light,
the Holy Spirit.
Some enlightened people help the lower,
slower vibrating people but God helps us all.

You must consciously seek the Spirit of God
because your soul can get distracted from its path.
You use your brain, body, your emotions
and senses,
but not your soul, your heart and your Spirit.
It's easy to get distracted on Earth
but you must follow the path
that your Spirit has chosen before birth.
A lot of time and thought is wasted
in frivolous gossip, stories and addictions.

Travel and variety in your surroundings
will let the Spirit feed you and teach you your lessons.
Time allows things to happen to you
that you cannot control, for the Great Spirit controls all.
In this way, your ability to serve the Spirit Family
may work itself out.
Attractions are made... a calling from within.
Situations may come about as an accident
or a thought driven process
and your loving and peaceful reaction to the world
makes all the difference in your lifetime.
Peaceful, forgiving acts
will raise your Spirit's level of vibration.

Plan on feeding your Spirit everyday!
Practice raising your own vibration to a higher level.
Attract yourself to the next highest high
of loving thoughts.
Then perfectly, love will surround you and attract to you.
Act in love and reach out in love
and love will reach into you and love will return to you.

Love yourself enough
to let the great Spirit of love shine into your heart
and love will shine through you from above
for all people to gain.

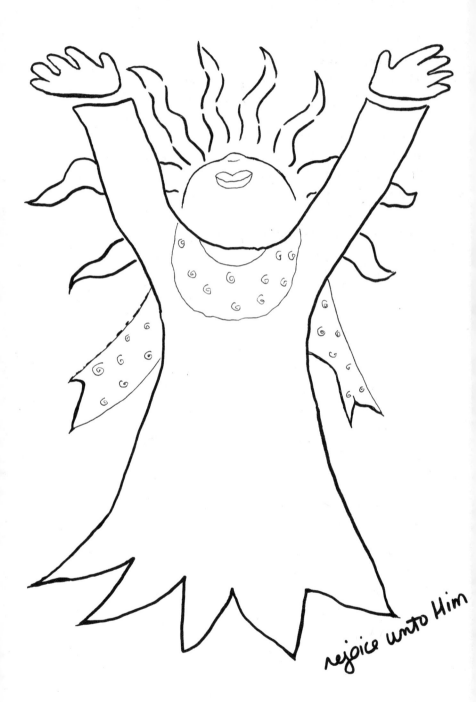

rejoice unto Him

The Rebirth

Mold my eyes to see the dawn,
a different way each early morn.
That I may walk the path of goodness
and leave behind all hours of sadness.

Hold my hand with gentle grace.
Replace the youthfulness of my face.
That I may pass the path of dusk
and tread deep into your night I trust.

Remove my narrow-mindedness.
Forgive my dreams of self-righteousness.
That I may walk your paths of light
and leave behind all memories that blight.

Mold my soul, Oh gentle Lord
to make it live by love, not sword.
Mold my heart, blessed by your loving sight,
your grace reborn in me tonight.

Blink of an Eye

What if in a blink of an eye
within an infra-second of time
you were suddenly released from the hardship of Earth.
You are suddenly free of all wants and all burdens...
you are instantaneously ejected from
the material, physical world and

14

you end up…where?
With what as your future?
With what as your measure?

In a flip of a switch, in one breath of an angel,
you are propelled to forgive yourself
for all of your physical crimes.
All those slights to relive,
burdens that haunt the earthly.

How can you make the transition easier?

Spirit says, open your spiritual gift.
Free yourself of the need for all material things
and longings by feeding your Spirit while on Earth.
Do good to all freely and often.
Think of light and love as you go on each day and
God will meet you at the pearly gates.

You know the treasures are inside your Spirit,
not within your body,
not within any physical part of Earth or object.

Your treasure is that piece of you that lives
throughout all of eternity
the DNA * seed * soul * heart
freed upon life's sweet departure.

Perhaps to return to Earth,
perhaps to join God forever.

Always,
yes always,
in a blink of an eye.

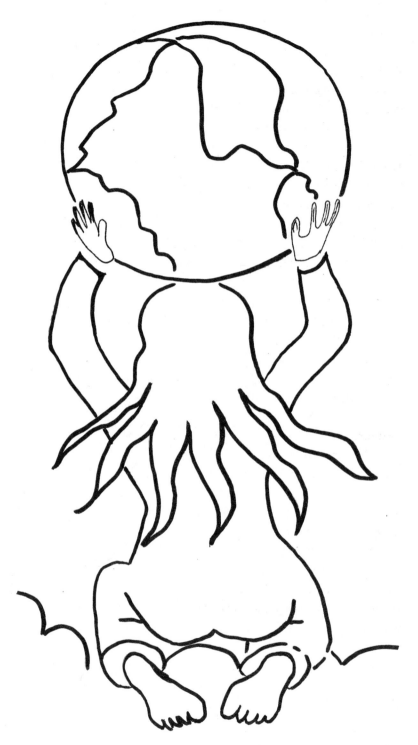

Women

Women,
whom I have treasured.
Friends who held my weak hand
while growing to my present state.

They chose each
their separate road to tread
but intermingled with my views and
my life with swift, relentless
intensity...
carving their images deep into my heart.

Beautiful faces that laugh and linger,
lonely faces that shared a female's plight.

Women who were not afraid to love.
No,
not like Earth men.

Women,
their love eternal
shared with me, all soul bared.

They bleed tears inside me,
droplets that ripple
through time.

Never be afraid to love, my child
for love is the only right action to
renew your heart's mission.

The Fading Rose

the fading rose sings
so quietly,
silently, wilting
her heart

small leaves bound together
stitched with
invisible thread to a
stalk
full of thorns yet
the life
pulses through it

to open the bud
a life short-lived
dying
as the seed does sprout

but the joy gathered
lingers and
the opening is not
in vain

Silent Tears

Hearts bleed
in silent circles,
meekly crying to neighbors
who wear walkmans
tuned to their saddest songs.

Those that do not cry,
hide
deep in rivers,
small stones of inadequacy,
polished to a magnificent glow.

Beware,
those that do not bleed.
Weights like those of Atlas
bear heavy on the soul.

Seek refuge in each other's arms.
Seek companionship from above.
Seek forgiveness for yourself always.

Holidays

Holidays are designed for gold ink pens
to say those words I never say.

But oh, I shouldn't let a day go by
without saying how much your touch has meant,
to say how much your image means
of times remembered and infinitely stored
amongst my treasures of pure gold memories.

Ones that should stay locked away,
that make me tremble for fear of time
so lightly spent.

Memories that make me tremble and wish it back,
to add one look, one word of love
to let you know again
how much you really mean to me.

And though time goes by, it still stays clear,
for time so lightly spent,
the light burns bright
to guide me back
and be there with you again.

And who would think such a precious memory
would come from that carefree moment!

Believing Makes It Real

Alternative to Realism

I'd rather believe in a lifetime of happiness,
in the eternal truth granted from a loving Creator,
in loving embraces I receive from all dimensions,
in laughter that induces great comfort to my heart,
in comfort ascending to all races but
back to realism again.
Back to the Earth.

If you'd rather believe in happiness,
and in truth
then let your soul shine,
let it shine right through your skin!

Believe!
It's not that hard to believe in goodness and joy
and striving to give your light away.

Believe! You will change the planet
with the gifts you bring to Earth!
You will be a living light!

Just take that corner of the world
right where you stand and
never
give
up.

Give to others what you lack and
you will get what you dream.
Forget the circumstance of your Earth life.
Know in your heart you are Lords of the Universe...
only a little lower than the angels and
a Blessed Child of God.

The Fountain of Life

The fountain of life
continues to pump its flow through me and to me,
without ever ceasing,
without ever faltering,
without ever assuming I am full,
without my consent and without my fear…

I accept my life's waters, power and energy…
for I am the pond where the fountain begins and ends.
I am the flow, the stream, the ocean and the raindrop.
I am the receiver, the giver, the benefactor and
the abundant one.

I am grateful for the universal life force
and its flow to me from the four corners of the universe.
I am grateful for the abundance I absorb everyday
from the forces around me.

I drink in all I touch.
I breathe in all I am sent.
I receive on all levels and in all dimensions of my being.

And I say thank you, Great Spirit.
I accept this life and these gifts.
I acknowledge more blessings to be forthcoming.

The fountain of life is my eternal blessing,
desiring to fill me more than I desire to be filled,
providing more abundance for me
than I can possibly receive.

I am spiritually, mentally and physically
full of love, light, peace and abundance.

ahhh.... winter ice

Christmas

Christmas is sunshine to all hearts
who choose to open and shut with time.
Hearts that rhythmically blacken after
the tinsel and ornaments have been stored away,
indicating the withdrawal of love and good cheer.

A white Christmas can be a blizzard of snow,
where angel tears crystallize
into a million different starlets,
starlets falling on the Earth.
A constant flow after the outdoor lights
have been returned to a box in the attic,
a vast storm of mournful frozen teardrops.

The heart of Christmas should be here all year long,
bringing generosity and joy to all the Earth.

For it is only humans who choose
to ebb and flow
inventing one season of loving…
never seeing more to the joy of Christmas
than a commercial decoration…
never letting the soul of Christmas in.

Behold your mission!
Bring the spirit of love into your heart and
hold it there.
Then you must share your heart with all the others!
Let love glow and twinkle and give you a new life.
Love was never meant to be stored in a box.

Purposes

Your purpose is known, deep in your dreams.
Deep in your heart, you know all things.

See the door to your peace open wide and beckon.
Envision your dream. Be truly self-respecting.

In details so vivid, your mission is revealed.
There is nothing in your soul meant to be concealed.

And the inklings? You'll feel them!
Seek your purpose now, with no rejecting.

Be brave in life's maze.
Pursue each dark road with the light of your heart.
Help with each heavy load.

Don't fret if you don't find your way,
as quickly as you thought you would.
Know in your heart the world is perfectly unfolding,
quite the way it should!

Brighten each face that you meet in the night.
Your purpose will be known with the dawning light.

32

Angel

Angel, hold the ladder,
the climb is very high.

Travel close beside me,
always look me in the eye.

Help me climb each rung with laughter,
always looking to the sky.

Having faith in God, Beloved,
we'll be reunited when we die.

Whisper in my ears loudly,
don't forsake me when I cry.

Angel, hold the ladder,
with your wings my soul can fly!

Ride the Rainbow Of Life

Races of Earth

Tempura batter covers us.
Spirits encased, like vegetables transformed.

Mutant skins and pasteurized oils,
placing masks of taste over our true being.

Colors of cherry and chocolate,
banana, olive
and cauliflower.

Earth collects miracles
and life weaves intricate patterns,
and mind creates incredible physical disguises
so you can't see
through the breading,
through the hollandaise,
through the butterscotch syrup and
into the egg whites.

Masquerading Spirits on parade
and the hot oil spatters on all...

Look closely at the mind mutations and
learn to live above them.

Grandfather Dream

We were all dressed up in our Sunday whites.
The banquet hall was empty except
for our party of three,
my Grandfather, my Mother and me.

And we danced and danced the night away
like we had never done in life.
And the show,
the entertainment show
was of flowers blooming... gladioluses.

Millions and millions of flowers.
Blooming and dying, blooming and dying,
and it was so beautiful, breathtaking,
a collage of colors and love and nature.
Just a breathtaking show.

And I turn to see my Grandfather's eyes
turn white in their sockets.
And I cry because I loved him so.
And we never really danced together.
No.
Not once.

But the flowers,
oh, we saw the flowers together.
The cycle of life.
The cycle of life.

Seize the day !

Peace of Mind

My life is shortened by turmoil and worry.
A torrid of wild thoughts that descend so ever slowly,
then rush like a flood into my brain.

Manmade thoughts laced with glass ceilings.
"You can't do that." "You are not smart enough."
"You are not fast enough."
Programmed thoughts of the past sent
to consume my positive mind and feelings.
Yet, I am the one who thinks!

Be gone, time and mind!
that yield to that awful rush of uncertainty.
I change my attitude and check in with Spirit.
I am the one who thinks. *I can* detach from my past.

I observe old beliefs and patterns falling
to the wayside of my footpath,
no longer applicable to me and my dream.
Old beliefs I held so real and true,
so full of false thought and temporary worldly opinion…
those thoughts I leave behind as I travel down
the paths of change never to return.

I live in the present moment. I walk in my truth.
I follow my spiritual path of light each morning.
I anticipate a smooth highway of bright times ahead.
I receive slowly, carefully selected thoughts
granted to me by a serene God while
He watches over and guides me.
I persist towards my ultimate destiny,
my ultimate purpose,
through trials of distraction,
through avalanches of obstacles
and into peace of mind.

Believe

Love and hope shall prevail in my life.
While on earth, I know not truth.
I know not reality.
I know not the beating drum and its sound,
the grim reaper and his clock
or why the painful day to day life...
I know not why the crowded streets...
the impure water...
or clouded skies for I have forgotten the truth.
I know nothing of the wind swept touch of feathers,

the true light,
the reasons for continuing.

I am ignorant of the true world around me
because it is invisible and perfect
not the chaotic world I see.

I know not myself, though I am a seeker of myself.
But I know I must choose to believe.

My beliefs become my truth;
my truth becomes my reality.
The reality of the sound of my beating heart,
the drumming of the love-keeper of time,
insuring me that as long as it beats
love and hope
will always prevail in my daily life.

It all starts within me.
I create my reality.
And I wander the crowded streets in polluted air ...
I am isolated in this body.
I know nothing of this earthly world
but I know
I must believe
and walk my path
with purpose and
without fear.

Without fear,
I believe in universal love and hope
and I wish this great peace,
may rain down upon you
also.

Isolated

I feel my Spirit drive my body...
pushing to get out of this muscle and bone cage
and I have a great need to feed my spiritual side.

I want to reach out on a daily basis
for the spiritual truths I need to console my soul.
The best ways known to man are
meditation, prayer and silence.
I connect and listen to that still small voice of
my Creator who loves me and never leaves my side.

Because in my Earth life, I can be left alone,
alone to feel isolated and different from all the others.
I feel like rebelling against all material things
and I feel I am just someone else's thoughts
distorted into and trapped inside my body.

Sometimes my body won't let my Spirit out!
The body's hold is so immediate and grounding,
instead of saying
"Today I go in search of my spiritual gifts and purpose."
I hear,
I can dance like this... move - move - move.
I can play ball like an athlete... run - throw - catch.
I want to love with my body but I want to tell you all,
love is in the Spirit, not in the flesh.

The only lasting satisfaction is in one's higher self,
the One above who is united in all,
never separated from us
for any reason, thought or feeling,
that universal inside of us.
For I tell you,
when I am one with the Great Spirit and my mission,
I have access to all the riches on the Planet.

43

Tell OTHERS how much you love them

The Road Ahead

Live and guide to your heart inside.
Let hatred go. Watch sunsets hide.

Your Spirit is here for you to grow.
Your purpose here, your heart does know.

Travel light
you'll need every drop of strength
to climb your mountaintop.

You can only wish
to exhume a holographic memory box.

Caterpillars eat and turn
to butterflies in the new age.

Beyond death,
you'll have form not.
You are only Spirit in higher elevations.

Winds of Desire

My soul is the boat.
My Spirit is the sail.
My desire is the wind.

Shear desire powers this endless life force
behind my soul and Spirit
sailing me into infinity on the Earth plane.

Winds of desire that begin somewhere…
and finish some equally far distance from here,
with no beginning and no end… just intensity.

My desire fuels the incredible force of hope
and direction in my soul
sometimes against the sea current of reason,
forcing the taunt stretch of each last rope of faith,

testing each fibrous thread and tie of persistence.
And yet my desire propels me to my dreams…
feeling each curved plank of me in stress,
clutching my bare morals as
the boat of my soul is tossed and turned over the waves.

What if the sail of my Spirit gives way?
The winds of desire could cause my Spirit to fail…
to rip and fly about
carefully abandoned,
mistakenly glad I am free in the wind, yet unable to sail
thus my soul set adrift, aimlessly lost…

This could happen at any second,
if my mind so desires,
if my heart loses its way.

It is as if my desire *must* test my Spirit's sails
in order for my boat-soul
to reach its golden shores of purpose and success.

So keep strong my Spirit,
let each tie and rope be re-tied and my sail catch
the gale wind, again and again,
on my journey to my dream.

Let each desire have a beginning
and an end
with a safe harbor for resting
and yet my soul
not anchored and rotting
but somehow
finding my purpose in the journey.

Ode To Wandering Spirits

Leave your troubles behind
Follow your higher mind
Have faith wherever you go
Dream and let joy be the seeds that you sow
Ask and hope shall come your way
Pray and be grateful of receiving today
Love deeply and seek peace wherever you roam
Be a true friend and you'll never wander alone.

48

Acceptance

Wishing for things that are not
Elephants
sit dreaming
shorter trunks they could have had,
somewhere in past evolution,
if only, if only
gray wrinkles weren't hereditary.
If only, peanuts grew in Africa,
but peanuts do not grow there!
Accept yourself and find your spiritual gift
here and now
instead of wishing for things that are not,
unless your vision
is to make
the world a better place.

Within

I am within Earth life.
Spirit life is within me.
Earth life is my surrounding force.
Spiritual life forces are alive in me.
Within this life, I make my own life.
My life is a product of my own feelings and thoughts.

Within Earth life, I am molded by my positive thoughts.
Spiritual life shapes me, forming my heart within.
Within life, I attract
all I have set out to achieve.
I select those people, those objects
to enter, to penetrate my life,
within life.

Within Earth life,
I must find and use my special spiritual gift
that withstood the transition
of my Spirit coming to Earth, the grounding.
For this gift provides the stepping-stones to my direction,
my purpose and my connection to my spiritual life,
within life and
also my life within;
the life within my heart.

Once found, hence with ease
my Spirit grows within me, around me, about me.
I ride the wave of life to the shore,
forever within Earth's grasp,
but what a joyful adventure!
To break free
means to break out of this body and
freely choose again,
my spiritual gift of life I'll have
within.

Living Today

If you knew what lay ahead,
you may never move from bed.
Grey days are not foretold,
unlike the setting sun of old.
So look not forward
or at yesterday's pain.
Live this moment with love,
as there is no other
and you will have not lived in vain.

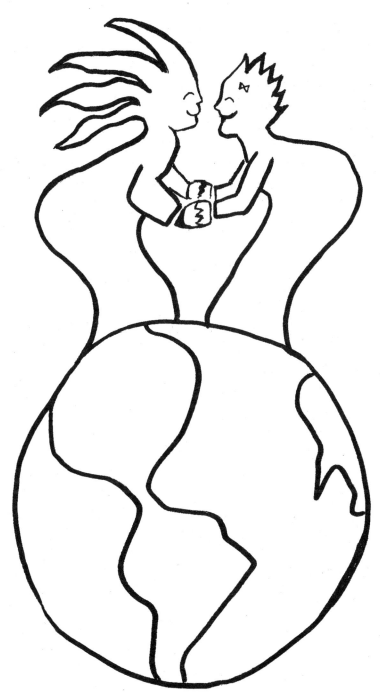

EARTH Welcomes SPIRIT

Mother Earth

For all the boundaries and limitations
you present on my Spirit,
I am a servant at your will – Mother Earth.

Not only am I caught in the beautiful and
deceptive qualities of my five senses
while under your beautiful sky
but I also race against the emotional pull
of feelings and other earthly distortions,
that breed my sins and vices.

And in growing this far,
I have learned the ways of the Earth.
I have learned I may rise up and fight
against others here or I may walk placidly
amidst the noise and haste.

I was granted a free will for my stay on Earth and
I will choose to use it to preserve the nature and
earthly beauty left to me by my forefathers.

I will pledge to Earth my true admiration
of her animal life and vegetable life.
I love her wondrous skies and her variety of colors.
I know the Earth is the substance composing my body.
She used the fine dust and seawater
of her elegant shores, her encasement particular
to my spiritual likeness of God.
But I am not all you see before you.

For it is clear,
I am above the mere creatures
that scramble and burrow along in the Earth.
Therefore, for my stay on Earth,
for whatever reason I am here and

however long I stay,
I will promote peace
among the warriors of this planet.
I will promote freedom of religion and ideas.
I will promote love between the continents.

Oh Earth, of earthly treasures,
let your images and substances not taint my soul,
or keep it from its goals
for I see within your splendor
the chains of greed and passing pleasures and
the acquisition of materials unnecessary to living my gift.
They are here only to distract me,
so let me not forget my true purpose.
I will be for a United Earth.

While on Earth,
each person feels so alone and isolated,
experiencing only their needs and only for their own sake.
I propose to each man to try to feel for his brother,
to feel for his brother's needs and comforts and
to live side by side with all people,
people who were all originally created equally
to live on Earth.

The reason for my present stay is not clear
but I hope to see through the physical embodiments
of people and objects and to see their true value,
shining out from their prison,
each captured within the grasp of matter.

For all physical features are but disguises
to steer me ever farther away
from Spirit's true virtues,
my Earth-lessons to be learned and from my final salvation.

55

The visions and emotions experienced by the Earthborn
are just foolish reasons to separate and
down-trod others who are
truly no different than myself.
They are just people in need of love and understanding.

Oh, Earth! Your gravitational hold of man
is so heavy and deadening!
This entrapment truly seems a
harsh punishment to my Spirit!

But I shall better my Spirit because of you!
Ha, ha Earth! I will use you to achieve physically
what I know is true spiritually!

For it is within this human form that I must see
that all humans are equal in God's eyes
and that every person is in need of love.

This is the reason that all inhabitants of Earth
should pursue friendship and kindness.
This is the reasoning that will allow me,
in my lifetime to see all the Earth's nations lay
down their swords and political walls and live,
truly live by the virtues of the Spirit,
here on Earth as they do in heaven.

The greatest reason
for the gift of free will in mankind
is because the fruits of the Spirit including
love, patience, joy, peace, faith, gentleness, kindness,
goodness and self-control
are *not of this Earth* and do not exist
on any mountain, ocean or plain
without a human heart to bring them to life!

Mother Earth – she is the final love test
we must pass to return to God,
and uplift the entire universe!

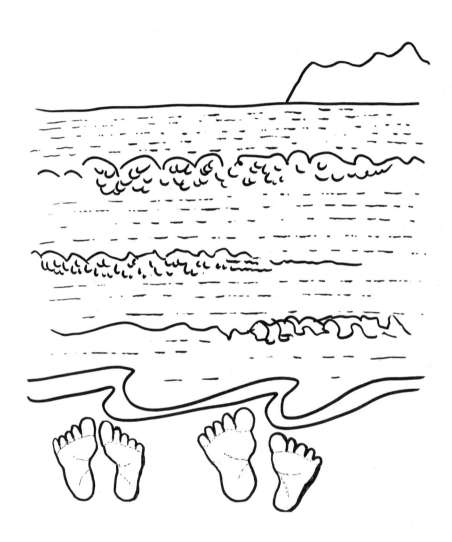

Earth Person

Drifting
dragging one foot
I crave for the silver bus to come
and I
with my backpack
will step aboard and
roll on to the future
stylishly
the "somewhere" I should be now
wandering the countryside
in search of my soul
my country and friends
I haven't met yet
and I'll dream of paradise
where all of the world loves one another
where no boundaries
neither land nor personal
interfere with our feelings of community
I live in a unified world
and I am a traveler
welcome everywhere

Grief

So rarely
does the gray bird sing.
So broken hearted...
my ears do ring!
Great sorrow only
do sweet notes bring.
So beware
the gray bird
when he sings.

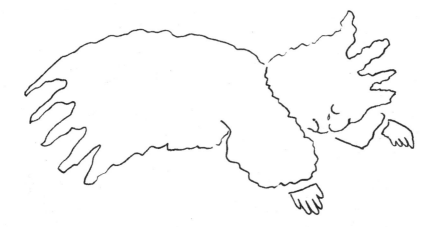

Get it all out
and move on...

Death

Dark black leaves of autumn fall.
Whirling feathers
of black crow call.

Rising temperatures
of an ozone destroyed,
no cold left for little girls and boys.

Pollution kills our Earth life
spreading a terminal waste.
Land never to regain God's sense of pure taste.

It is a plain waste of good molecules when
the endangered fowl,
lie dying in oil trenches and
not by the claw of the owl.

Ebony blazes intake the forests,
dry with the blood of only God's poorest.

Death approaches one and all.
Whether it is justice or
a cycle of life that we fall.

Death cutting free
our sense of responsibility.

But tell me
who are Earth's children
if not ourselves?

Father Time

Master Enemy, Master Time,
let me live something of a precious life,
something honest, gold of hue
that sands can't waste a second of.

"Oh, don't believe them!" Enemy cried.
"I am always on your side!"
Hands that turn and hands that hide.
Around his face hands fly.

See those clock watchers running all around.
See families trampled to the ground.
At five o'clock every eye looks your way,
but you've taken more than just their day.

Time is just coincidence,
fated moments always falling into place.
Can you live without the money, the monkey, the latchkey?
Escape the earthly rat race?

"Time freedom" is written on your wish list.
Run! Don't waste a good-by kiss.
Faster! Just stick with what you know…
Father Time, as quickly as you come, you go.

Earth Spirit's Dance

When the Earth shakes...
rolling like thunder,
an ocean wave
under my house.

I see God
looking down
and us all
looking up
to the fickle finger
of the vibrations.

I feel the Earth Spirit's dance,
her resentment released for now,
escaping
like prisoners into the fresh air.

Mother Earth
lets us
live here on the edge
of paradise.

Never be too sure
she will let us remain.

War

In ancient times
they killed their young
by sending them off to war.
Death would not be a tragic loss
as long as you had more.

Wishing to remain alive
and a tribute to one's race,
the Generals send away a million souls
and cut off their nose to spite their face.

In recent times, we still see war and
the young folks whose families pay.
And time remains, yet revokes,
its nameless saving grace
as the only cure
for a pain that won't go away.

The war rages in the spiritual plane
so it's a necessity that you care.
The solution is a spiritual one,
evolution of the ability to share.

Greed and dishonesty
can't replace the peace we bear.
Turn your back on the evil one
for in love, not war
all is fair.

Save the Trees

Please don't cut the trees down anymore.
There won't be enough earth to hold down the soil.
There won't be enough shade to beat down the heat.
There won't be enough branches of fruit left to eat.

Please don't cut down the trees.
It means so much to me,
to look high in the sky and see the green limbs that climb…
to see eagles nest up, to see pine needles fall down,
to feel oxygen built around a forest floor…
We must ask for more, oh please, plant some more!

We can't live in homes if we cut down the trees
or read or write books, only e-mails please.
Recycle those papers, boxes and cans.
Help save every tree and increase protection demands.
Go ride in the forest and take your children too.
Show them the old growth forest before they're cut down too.
There should be a stand taken up for the trees!
They're still given by God, grown with love and for free.

Profess your love now, if only they'll hear.
Protect all trees over 10-feet high
and require each person to plant a new tree each year.
Don't cut all the big branches off.
Let the 4-inch or larger branches stay.
Why do we let the chainsaw boys go to town and
wreck our shade? We should have a say.

It's not a joke to choke on smoke.
We must pass new tree laws and save the Earth and big trees
for ourselves and our little folk.
By the vote, we all share this land,
but I have to say,
I have no saw in my hand.

Childhood Friends

I recognize a familiar voice.
Images flash of times long, long ago.
Feelings rise to respond to that familiarity
and my pulse quickens, suddenly
I am there with you! My childhood friend!

At some point in life,
you forsake those dear friends
you haven't heard from ever again.
A scratch in your telephone book,
out of touch but not totally out of mind.

The connection still pulses between hearts
except you may recall it not.
And when you look into each other's eyes,
it may seem as though nothing has changed
or come between your hearts
although you were apart for many years.
And you say inside,
"I'm so glad you remember me, as I remember you.
A friend who wondered where the bonds went,
where the dreams go.
I wondered if any one of us had made it to their dream.
Oh, youthful dream!
That distant purpose we pursued together,
that haunted us and drove us so much in our youth."

And I hear your answer,
"Oh, my friend, I remember. I remember too!
and those purposes, those dreams haunt me still...
And we could never have known all the roads ahead
or not to fall in love so young.
No one told us, not to accept temporary things
as so permanent and lasting.
Everything is changing everyday, my friend.
Because it is the bond of time that we share,
those times so sweet, not the reality at hand."

So let us enjoy our youthful times and shining moments,
those divine memories with friends, new and old!
Simply because we cannot return, no less speed ahead.
So shower those people who mean something to you
this minute with kindness and love *today*,
for your roads may never cross again.
And always remember,
their thoughts and yours *are still* intertwined in Spirit.
And while on Earth, you are only a phone call away.

How To Live

To love together and never forget
To give away and never regret
To dream and never limit your mind
To feel and never stop being able to cry

To hold a child and never hit
To care enough to never quit
To sleep in peace and never stress
To eat whole foods that God grows best

To seek your spirit and never stop
To commit to marriage and never shop
To earn your keep and never take
To speak the truth for truth's own sake

To work at what you love
To love the work you do
To create abundance from the air
To thine own self be true...
This is the life I wish for you!

The Ocean

Swells revealing,
tiny mounds.
Reflections ripple,
sapphire clouds.
Algae walls
fight back
Beneath,
the green sand
Billows
that break the reef.
Endlessly forging,
the tide winding its waves.
Pummeled and pardoned
to drive sandcastles away.
But she calls, oh so softly
the crashes rhythmic to my ear.
The sweet ocean beckoning,
the sand naked with fear.

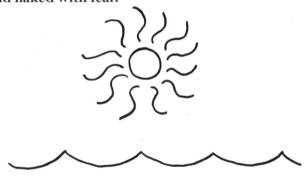

The Promise

Mother,
we made a bond between us,
a promise,
two spirits intertwined in destiny.

In all good time
we would teach each other our purpose.
We would grow each other's gifts of the Spirit.

I would give up my life for yours,
and you would give up your life for mine.

In each life, we trade and now,
it is your turn to live without me.

The circumstances of this life
will be to your benefit.
Therefore, as man offers the ability to
let a woman own her body,
Mother chooses the road
from which she can never return.

Thank you, Mother
for keeping your promise.
I love you evermore for that.

I Knew True Love

Inevitable
that your eyes glow
caught fire by love
in its first,
most passionate form.

I feel the tentacles of desire envelop me
casting off all life and sound about me
except
your stunning eyes
that beckon and seem
so full of life,
so gentle and giving.

I am captured for an instant...
I blush,
embarrassed
forced to look away
but the flame was there
so true to life,
holding my existence
for one second in time at bay...
For that infinite second...
I knew true love.

Love Secrets

Secrets
fall brilliantly from the sky
two people
watch gathering those fallen ones
together
sharing moments over
smoldering rocks
using sticks
careful not to touch
each looking into each other's eyes
they bury each rock
hoping, praying for it to cool
hands laid over the Earth
feel the heat
trails of meteors burning
in their eyes
reasons for meeting
Love secrets of the sky

Loneliness

How lonely is the life we lead
enclosed within
no mercy

Not a shadow of a friend to heed
a bleeding, emotional
man-child-girl
Experiencing torture
compared to the next world

Aches that invade me
deep in sound sleep
blistering

festers
boils of loneliness seep
Sweating sacks of blood
shedding skin
eyes so black

Eyes so black
Oh, Great One who made this school for Spirits
call me back
call me back

How lonely is the earth life we lead
sounds of silence
echo through me

Sky Lights

Remember when the sky lights of heaven
made you sit back and feel so connected?

A hole in the universe to gaze into...
the ultimate vastness that gave you wings...
to see those loving eyes
far away,
but you envisioned them clear as day
and the sky light reflected from their eyes
back to you and your eyes,
instantaneously
you and your soul mate connected in the moonlight
while looking into the deepest universe,
while looking into the wild midnight moon.

This universal light shines out to me like the sun
into my winter heart.
Something to revolve around...
light that awakens me and catches my Spirit on fire.
This same light is in my soul and yours
and in the dreamer's eyes.
It is in the sparkling stars of heaven
and in all human hearts.
This beautiful light shines deep within my Spirit body
and every atom of my being
glows with lightness and peace when I feel it within.

Oh, I remember well, getting lost in the sky lights...
as I sit back and dream
up to the heavens,
out to the four corners of the universe or
into your eyes.
The fruits of the Spirit guide me on this journey and
I am one
with all my Spirit family.

Relative Worries

I cringe at the mirror side.
After the midnight run my eyes look
black and hollow.
My hair is falling out.
My clothes are wearing out,
my tapes are stretched,
my CD's break and skip.
My eyes need glasses,
my double chin appears.
Fake teeth, fake smiles, where's the bleach?
Worries of no necessity –
just the way the body is.

I should worry as much
about knowing myself!

For it seems so evident
I am not my body.
My body is not my purpose.
I am born into this world with nothing and
I shall leave with nothing.
Since my Spirit is my only constant
within Earth and sky
perhaps I am here to discover and
know my Spirit and
learn to reconnect
with my Spirit family,
my spiritual gifts
and my purpose I am to bring to Earth.

What a concept!

OPEN YOUR ARMS
accept Yourself

Eye Embraces

Your love could come and stay here
deeply embossed, wrapped and set
into my folded heart...
a gem to glow and give off strange light,
a love like mortals have never seen on Earth...

and I'd envelop your love
like the foil on a chocolate,
folded
around this precious gift, gently
protecting,
embracing,
believing
it feels right inside.

If you'd only give the signal,
the look,
allow the true story to begin...
the true passion to begin...
You must give your love to begin...

A strange emptiness embraces me
like the new moon in a starry sky
because this ring I desire,
with your love as the gem and
my heart as the setting,
never comes to bear,
for you turn your head and look away.

Plant Life

Where are the roots of spiritual life in the universe?

Are fingers found within the trelliswork
of the towering stars
that dot the sky?

Are buds and seeds entangled within the rocks,
shallow pools and lower ripples of the mountain stream?

Are branches of fruit budding behind your eyes
enhancing your vision toward the aspects we need to share?

Are there tiny sprigs of starter seedlings
sprouting in your heart then carefully
blossoming around each new
emotional experience
as the sun sets every day?

Each human spark
is a vine of universal life
that grows along the Earth
in hopes of finding something solid
to grow upon.

Where is the arbor of the Universe?
Where is it and on what framework will
we all grow together?

Find your xylem and
let us seek
the most beautiful of worlds
together.

A Loving Thought

If everyone were happy where they were,
there would be no turmoil,
no longing or roaming.

If everyone were happy about their lives,
there would be no need for
"higher" education, class systems or stealing.

If everyone were happy about themselves,
there would be no aerobics classes,
no psychotherapy and no cults
and if everyone were happy they lived on one planet, Earth,
there would be no war, no prejudice and no suicide.

But instead of satisfaction and gratitude for our chosen path,
we find discontentment.
Instead of peace of mind with purpose, we find disharmony.
Instead of love for each other, we find apathy.

The purity of this Earth
has been poisoned with liars, the love of money,
power mongers and television.

Create in your own mind a clear vision of yourself
as a peaceful, grateful, perfect and
whole spiritual being learning to give
your gifts of light with love
and forgiveness to the physical world.

Let us all lift the darkness.

Think a silent, clear, loving thought
and project it on the world and your Spirit family,
right now
for 11 seconds.

Letter to my Children

Dear Children,
Teach by example. Love unconditionally
and know it is never too late to learn to love or teach.

If just one child learns determination and diligence...
he will find all possible faith within adversity.
You will achieve what others call "the unachievable".
They will lead many to easily rebound from failure.
Be determined in your Spirit. Never give up hope.

If just one child seeks their wildest dream...
he will have captured the great spirit of youth for a lifetime.
You will find love in Spirit, mind and body.
They will bring many gifts from the Stationary Mind
onto the Earth by living their purpose.
Seek your childhood dreams! Let your Spirit come to Earth.

If just one child keeps courage in his heart...
he won't fear the uncertainty of the journey through time.
You will allow bad times to pass and expect better.
They will know in their heart that all is just as it should be.
Strive to keep courage in your heart!

If just one child understands time and patience...
he will be quiet and level-headed in havoc.
You will allow seasons and people to move at their own rate.
They will seek and learn their own true nature. What a gift!
Learn and teach patience. Seek to understand time.

If just one child enjoys the present moment...
he will carry a smile and enjoy life's adventures.
You will find joy and peace in today's journey.
They will make the best of each moment as given.
Enjoy the present moment with all its adventures!
Seize the day! Be happy and joyful for your daily gifts.

If just one child pursues life with unrelenting persistence...
he will keep focused on his purpose and spiritual gifts.
You will be gentle in your actions, thoughts and deeds.
They will bring much faith and hope to Earth and to this life.
Cultivate unrelenting persistence and burning desire.

If just one child honestly praises another person...
he will gain humility in himself.
You will see another's goodness over their faults with ease.
They will lift others to do great things and
make lasting friendships.
Give praise lovingly, freely and kindly.

If just one child feels empathy in his heart for another...
he will live a life of gentleness and kindness.
You will think ahead to the consequences of your actions.
They will live in harmony with the Earth and their fellow
humans and rarely need to apologize or regret.
Strive to live in consideration of your Spirit Family.

If just one child learns to love and respect himself...
he will project equality and have respect for others.
You will gain self-control and the respect of others easily.
They will lead a life full of goodness and lift us all!
Learn to love and respect yourself.

Children, above all else,
teach each other how to love the Earth and everyone in it.
Pray for spiritual peace and the deliverance of mankind
and claim a higher calling for yourself and your children.
Give to the children of the world
all your kindness and all your encouragement,
for each life ripples far in its sphere of influence.
*Thus your gifts return to Earth through your Spirit and
your children's Spirit for all the years to come!*

My Eyes

If I saved every scrap
of impulse that went
into my system,
my brain,
my outlook...

it could take a million years
to create,
or recreate
what I do and did
so naturally
as my life unfolded,

and even then
you would never know
the correct intensity,
the bitter sweetness,
the hidden view
only my eyes beheld,
or the incredible love
my heart has known.

Indelible as it may seem to my Spirit,
how correct for it
to be
just so.

My life is written in the Stationary Mind.
Do not doubt it for an instant.

Chasing Down a dream ...

Camel Dream

You are a camel out on the desert Earth.

The water that you have stored
leaves slowly, deliberately.

What is the motive for your slow wandering?
What is the purpose you fulfill?
Do you carry within you, your hopes and dreams?

Your hump stands tall,
a symbol of your gathered strength to survive
out on the dry hot sands of Earth.

Your long eyelashes guard your eyes from the winds.
Do not look upon the stinging sands
as a curse, but
your protection as an element of wonder.

Where I stand, I marvel at your confidence,
to walk where there is no path,
to adapt where there is no choice,
to travel a place where all others dare not.

I want to be a camel.
Let me not stray from my dream.

Neptune's Falls

In hopes of passing love's tests of inspection,
in hope of compassion, not glazing rejection.
I seek the peace of Neptune's falls,
within this place of love, Spirit calls.

Silently I peek to see,
Neptune's throne of abalone.
Pearls and bits of kelp and gold,
are reflected from his sea-cloak folds.

He sits atop a massive seashell
and oversees the ocean swells.
His throne built on dreams, coral reefs, ocean streams...
between his feet flow the life-force of Earth.

I see his hair long, flowing down.
He yields his trident and his crown.
King of all this watery ground,
Neptune's watch falls without a sound.

Behold, Neptune wishes on the morning star.
He radiates calmness and peace to lands and oceans far,
to all those fishermen nearby his sea,
that love the deep water as much as he.

And quiet invades the watery swill,
the sun rises gold on the distant hills.
Ocean waves scatter vibrating his peace and love,
the tide runs high, the morning star shines above.

And the fisherman on the distant shore,
woken early, gathers his lures,
casts his faithful boat out to the sea,
for what is found there was meant to be.

And he too, wishes on the morning star
as he begins his watch on the sandy bar,
drawn to the ocean he loves best of all,
he's found true peace near Neptune's Falls.

King Neptune's love surrounds the man,
filling his heart, truly touching his hand,
with secrets gained through silent eyes,
vibrations attracted,
sent as King Neptune's prize.

Within his heart he feels such connection,
his face beguiles a grin.
His eyes reflect a glimmer of a fish's silver fin.
The fisherman releases his catch
over the waves thundering crash.
The Earth's web of life
rules all men,
unsurpassed.

Lightness

Take away my impatience.
Take away my body.

If I shine so brightly clothed in this skin
there must be a light inside,
glowing, wishing to be set free.

The lightness within endures and awaits
the test of time,
free of turmoil yet yearning to let go.

In the night
before my head lies
peacefully with acceptance and duty
on the sheets,
I dwell into my spiritual mind;
into that higher masked person, that is my self.

I try to reach the lightness,
to experience it without thought.
I must be more than human;
I must live on forever.
I am surely part of the light that goes on forever!

Inside this earthly prison of fears and familiarity,
the light stands tall.
The strength is not dulled by my Earth transformation.

The lightness lives here in my soul,
among the Spirit family in the circle of eternity.
Lifting me in my every step and in every moment,
roaring for great peace and wholeness to return to me
and when my light is finally set free,
I will be one with all the universal light,
once again.

Only Dust

Separate my soul and body.
Take each one and measure its fineness;
One will be more fine.

You see only my body and measure it
and find flaws.
What did you expect?
It is flawed!

You flirt. You laugh.
You are only made of dust yourself.

Then, choose to view my soul as it truly is,
and marvel at the perfect, divided machine!

More refined than any physical form.
More connected than any telephone network.
Already existing in true perfection,
grace and beauty
yet I can hardly accept in my own mind that
right now
a part of me is timeless,
endless,
ever connected and eternal in the light.

I am more a part of the great universe and
universal design
than my earthly mind can
truly imagine or grasp.

What a wondrous gift
we are given
to explore, indeed!

Golden Threads

Each human life is a thread in the tapestry of Earth time.
Never fraying, each influence eternally present.

Each ego lives; then, as we know it, dies
and their memory may slowly fade in Earth time
but the golden threads of Spirit
are woven forever
into the universal tapestry and
only brighten and lighten the load of the whole.

These shining threads,
provide us all strength through love and giving deeds,
through positive thoughts, words and memories.
They teach us forgiveness and ignite the path
we follow with their encouragement.
Like a beacon in the darkest night,
their love shines bright and leaves the ego for dead.

Other threads over and under the golden ones
can't help but be crafted into their kindness and light.
We earth-bound are one of many segments
in the pattern of the universal tapestry.
We should not judge those Spirits
that fail to recognize a common chord,
a common basis beneath the surface.

Simply lift them!

What a monument to God and the heavens
we would be,
as a race to recognize,
the underlying human connection in the universe
and all the vast dimensions of Spirits
in great need of love and lifting!

Passing On

When someone you know is passing on,
don't be afraid; don't ask them to stay.
Ask God to let this Spirit enter his kingdom;
Ask God to heal this Spirit or
take him away from the Earth.
Only then will their soul dance and fly to
the highest vibration.

You wouldn't want the Spirit to stay here
if it meant surveying the earthly world while
wishing to return,
for that would only mean more suffering,
more useless objects to collect.

Think more central to your heart and soul.
Use your love for them.
Tell them you wish them love
and that you'll soon meet them on the other side,
reunited in all good time in heaven.

Tell them to follow the light and
not to worry about Earth.
Heaven is a much higher place.

Tell them,
"I am always with you.
I am connected to you.
I speak to you through Spirit and
I am glad you are released
from all your earthly
pain and tears and fears.
Have faith…
for that is the promise of God."

Eternity

The blank sheet awakens
to an earthly garden of lush purple flowers.
Oh, how the Spirit family freely gives its treasures and gifts
to those who love and seek to awaken and serve.

A life-body rises up from the ash;
A drop of moisture from an angel's tear;
A seed-Spirit from the heavens descends into form;
to a point, a star burst; Ahhhh… down the slide…

The dream begins;
A struggle to break the surface of reality
through the clouds of emotion and Earth;
A desolate walk through Earth-time;
Remembering to share your gift of Spirit and purpose;
Learning to give and to receive from each other;
Spreading joy and hope to each heart you meet;
but oh blessing!

A brilliant golden light flashes;
the balloon of body bursts open
and we fly into complete freedom from the darkness.

Only to return again to the Earth,
a flower bed,
a blank sheet.
A Spirit bound again to the
earthly garden of lush purple flowers
to perfect and lift your soul and
the others
one more time…

Long Song

Sing.
Sing a long song.
Sing it loud.
Forever till the sun burns out
be proud.
You are a piece of time,
just a piece of time.
All your life,
no matter what your mind,
just be you,
to yourself, be kind.

Sing.
Sing a long song.
Sing and shout!
Forever hold love in your heart
and laugh love out!
You are a piece of time,
just a piece of time.
All your life,
no matter what you do,
just be you,
to your soul be true.

Rag Doll

If you have doubts of your true self,
leave them behind.

You are a material doll within this world
given a loving heart, provided a computer-like brain,
blessed with the power of words,
having chosen an earthly purpose and
a spiritual gift to share.

When it comes time and
your seams are split and threadbare,
your familiar form will disappear
and crumble into the soft Earth.

And you will not be able to communicate
the same way as the Earth people who
still have their rag doll bodies.
Your love will live and remain on Earth
with those you loved,
but your essence of soul will float up to Spirit and
survey a Spiritual haven beyond compare
and you will return to live with your Spirit family again.

You will live again, my friend!
Only now, without the buttons and threads
that kept you puzzling whether
the extent of your being
was truly contained
within those
earthly
physical
boundaries!
Live your gift!
Don't waste a moment!

109

I Love The Earth

I love the Earth,
the angels who hover near cry.
We will help you,
move your heart to understand.

Only icicles for that frozen glow
that hangs above the cooling towers.
Orange mutants that lived through the fire
pray for a near fatal blast.

OOO mmm ooo fff.
AAAaaa uuuUUU MMMmmm.
Then silence.

Until the Angel,
the lone Angel of Earth and humanity
redeem them,
war and hell shall be present.

We must say it all together.
Humans must stand up and
accept the common links between us all!

Shout my people,
I love the Earth!
and we won't let you blow it up
and destroy our home!
I love the Earth!
Let us all begin to understand and
stand up
for universal peace, love and service.

Sometimes

I'll probably
always be
the person you see now.
I may not be too beautiful
but I'll make it through somehow.
And anytime
you need a friend,
remember I am here.
In my heart, our love is clear.
Although sometimes far away,
            sometimes so near.

I'll probably
always be
a gypsy in my ways.
I may not settle down
but I know I've seen my family days.
And loneliness,
she's been my friend,
remember if you care.
In that way, we all share.
Although sometimes far away,
            sometimes so near.

Method of Change

Time drifts by, captivating us.
Time brings on age and wisdom.
Wisdom instills compassion,
compassion brings peace to the Earth.

Time speeds by, amazing us.
Time grows our hearts and our children.
The capacity to love grows our patience
and patience grows into kindness and empathy.

Time travels by, enhancing us.
Time instills humility and faith.
Humility increases character
and character allows us to cultivate
great inner peace and strength.

With the wonderful things time can achieve,
it is our only method of change.
Should time be altered or stopped,
we would never know anything different
than a single stationary feeling.

So God invented time and Earth,
allowing you to express and live a million feelings.
Behold the birth and aging of a new civilization!
You can experience the journey of changes
in every second of your Spirit's existence on Earth.

God invented time on purpose...
just so He could count and chart
how many single moments in time you smiled
and under what circumstance
you gave out a happy thought,
a prayer of peace,
your helping hand given to others in the light of love.

Forever Friends

Forever friends are hard to find.
The kind that hang around
even when your down,
even when your afraid.

Forever friends are hard to come by.
The way they make you smile,
how special they make you feel.
They know that love is real.

Will you be a forever friend of mine?
Oh, in time, all things change,
don't they, don't they?
Say somewhere, say in time,
you'll be a forever friend of mine.

Forever friends, if you need me,
I'll stay within close distance.
Forever friends we'll be
when your down or afraid.

Forever friends are hard to find.
The kind that make you laugh,
that hold your heart in light.
They are your hindsight.

Will you be a forever friend?
Oh, in life all things change,
don't they, don't they?
Some say good-bye, but say in time,
you'll be a forever friend of mine.

117

The Spirit And the Earth

I am trapped here
on Earth!
Cried the Spirit.
Whatever should I do?

The Earth answered
with a gentle golden sunrise.

Live your gifts of reason.
Seek and know your purpose.
Share your spiritual gifts while on Earth.
Choose to make a positive difference.

Sow wisely,
because you shall reap
again and again,
forever
until the chain be broken.

For who are our children
if not ourselves?

The Stationary Mind

You are not your body.
You are a seed planted in your body
to sprout and grow sowing love.

Your higher mind is stationary inside you,
that eternal part that never is altered
and the world is all around distorting things,
providing trials and things to test you.
Why you don't even remember
what your existence is supposed to be like!

You are perfect in your design.
You are an educational, living, carbon, E-Ticket ride
for your special spiritual purpose in mind!
Created to perfect that non-rational,
invisible-to-this-place
part of your higher self.

You have the ability to pursue any trail on Earth.
Any ability may be yours with hard mental work and
practice in thought control.
Each small step of progress is forever etched in
the treasure chest of your higher mind.
Treasures that await the joyful adventurer;
you who recognize and share your confinement.
You who grow from the lack of spiritual air
unlike the others who just
give up and waste away.

We must give to each other like we
are all prisoners waiting to break free.
We must love each other,
for we are all the same in that Stationary Mind.
Each of our treasure chests are full of each of
our own deeds and thoughts.

We fill a treasure chest for each day.
What are your chests filled with, my friend?
What did you give to your fellow prisoners today?

You are a living, breathing, serving machine.
Everything you touch, smell, feel, think and intend
is for forever.
Each truthful breath, each sparkle of the eye
will fall forever within the Stationary Mind.
All is safe there. Love is contained there.
The energy is taken from each act and stored,
vitalized and concentrated.
It is stored in that part of yourself
you really don't know of, really.

That place you can't quite recall.
But if you only knew what joy there is
in filling each basket to the brim each day;
fulfilling each test with grace and patience!
If you only saw how superficial
life and its rules are, how fragile the veil
of Spirit is, how easy to slip over to the spirit side again!

A group of sparks expands after ignition and
scatters into the universe.
To be human is to be spiritually connected to all things.
Your Spirit is a part of everything,
everything you see and everything you feel.
If you learn to listen, there is nothing you do not know.

Somewhere in the collective unconscious
there rests a treasury of lives and experiences
which is accessible to every soul that seeks its purpose.
Seeking this connection in your life
is a part of your purpose!

The brothers of our spark,
each a segment of the whole
are waiting for you to remember your Spirit family.
You must experience this connection
to believe and remember *all you truly are.*

Your compassion must grow continually while on Earth.
For you *are* everyone, because in your Spirit
you are connected to everyone through the Stationary Mind!
And to forgive yourself,
you must forgive all others and
feed your heavenly treasure box with light.

You must forgive everyone
for their current lack of light and knowledge so
you may be freed and you must forgive yourself
for your current lack of light and knowledge
if you are to set others free.

This is a hard Earth-task to be sure... but it is the only way.
The way to the camp will be through the dense trees.

If you only knew how much joy was flowing to you,
how great this universal love meant to heal you!
How all these treasures await you, welcome you and
invite you to remember this place called Stationary Mind!
You would seek this gift all of your Earth days!

Live your specific Earth-purpose, here and now and
share your special-to-this-place spiritual gift!
Hence, with this remembered joy in your heart,
you can easily fill your life, thoughts and heart
with God's vast storehouse of love, abundance and peace.
For truly, I tell you, all of these treasures
are available to *you* each and every day!

... The Beginning of the journey
for Purpose and Meaning

POEM INDEX

Title	First Line	Page
Acceptance	Wishing for things that are not	49
A Loving Thought	If everyone were happy where they	91
Alternative to Realism	I'd rather believe in a lifetime of	25
Angel	Angel, hold the ladder	33
Believe	Love and hope shall prevail in my life	40
Blink of an Eye	What if in a blink of an eye	14
Camel Dream	You are a camel out on the desert	97
Childhood Friends	I recognize a familiar voice	72
Christmas	Christmas is sunshine to all hearts	29
Death	Dark black leaves of autumn fall	63
Earth Person	Drifting	59
Earth Spirit's Dance	When the Earth shakes	67
Eye Embraces	Your love could come and stay here	89
Eternity	The blank sheet awakens	107
Father Time	Master Enemy, Master Time	65
Forever Friends	Forever friends are hard to find	117
Golden Threads	Each human life is a thread in the	104
Grandfather Dream	We were all dressed up in our Sunday	37
Grief	So rarely	61
Holidays	Holidays are designed for gold ink pens	23
How To Live	To love together and never forget	74
I Knew True Love	Inevitable	79
I Love the Earth	I love the Earth	111
Isolated	I feel my Spirit drive my body	42
Letter to my Children	Dear Children	93
Lightness	Take away my impatience	101
Living Today	If you knew what lay ahead	52
Loneliness	How lonely is the life we lead	82
Long Song	Sing	108
Love secrets	Secrets	81
Method of Change	Time drifts by, captivating us	115
Mother Earth	For all the boundaries and limitations	54
My Eyes	If I saved every scrap	95
Neptune's Falls	In hopes of passing love's test of	99
Ode to Wandering Spirits	Leave your troubles behind	48
Only Dust	Separate my soul and body	103
Paradise on Earth	You should go about	6
Passing On	When someone you know is passing	105
Peace of Mind	My life is shortened by turmoil	39

Plant Life .... Where are the roots of spiritual life 90
Purposes .... Your purpose is known, deep in your 31
Races of Earth .... Tempura batter covers us 35
Rag Doll........................... If you have doubts of your true self 109
Relative Worries .... I cringe at the mirror side 86
Save the Trees.................. Please don't cut the trees down anymore 71
Silent Tears .... Hearts bleed 21
Sky Lights .... Remember when the sky lights 85
Sometimes .... I'll probably 113
Spiritual Attraction .... A Spirit should attract to itself 10
The Fading Rose .... The fading rose sings 19
The Fountain of Life .... The fountain of life 26
The Ocean .... Swells revealing 75
The Promise .... Mother 77
The Rebirth .... Mold my eyes to see the dawn 13
The Road Ahead .... Write and guide to your heart inside 45
The Spirit and the Earth ...I am trapped here 119
The Stationary Mind ...... You are not your body 120
War .... In ancient times 69
Winds of Desire .... My soul is the boat 46
Within .... I am within Earth life 51
Women .... Women 17

Illustrations Index   **Page**
Spirit Family dinner.. 1
Lollipop for Boy of Joy 3
Boy of Joy and Maya the Spirit Dog 5
Dolphin Paradise 9
Love and Gentleness - 2 Spirits attracting 11
Mama Love Spirit Rejoices unto Him 12
Butterfly Transformations 14
Sister Patience holds the world 16
Fading Rose 18
No one allowed 20
Grandma Goodness and Baby Kindness 22
Believing makes it real 24
Fountain Of Life (Boy of Joy) 26
Ahhh...winter ice (Boy of Joy) 28
Mama Love Spirit in the moonlight 30
Maya, the Spirit Dog of self-control 32
Ride the Rainbow of Life (Boy of Joy) 34
The Spirit Cmes to Earth Family Portrait 36
Seize the Day (Boy of Joy) 38
Spirit meditates 40
Dance, Dance, Dance 43

Illustration Index   Page

Tell others how much you love them............................44

The Kiss... 46

Honor each other (Mama Love Spirit and Baby Kindness) 48

Elephant with Boy of Joy Spirit..................................49

Reading in Bed...50

Helping Hand - Girl of Peace......................................52

Boy of Joy and Girl of Peace on top of the Earth................53

Boy of Joy Spirit Reads under a tree............................ 57

Down By the Sea - You and me..................................... 58

Falling Star (Mama Love Spirit)..................................60

Get it all out and move on (Baby Kindness)...................... 61

Sister Patience with Girl of Peace on lap...................... 62

The Clock (Girl of Peace).. 64

Earth Spirit...66

Falling Star (Mama Love Spirit).................................68

Boy of Joy hugs a tree... 70

Boy of Joy rides on Sled... 72

Girl of Peace and Boy of Joy laugh together......................74

Mama Love Spirit floating in the Ocean...........................75

Mama Love Spirit pregnant with Child.............................76

True Love (Daddy Gentleness and Mama Love Spirit) 78

Lightening Bolt (Daddy Gentleness and Mama Love Spirit)......... 80

Loneliness (Boy of Joy)...82

Joy and Maya Fishing..83

Stargazing..84

Open your arms and accept yourself (Boy of Joy).................. 87

Sun and Moon Spirit.. 88

The Arbor of the Universe...90

Kindness and Maya, baby and dog...................................91

Baby Kindness and Daddy Gentleness................................92

Through the eyes of Peace...95

Mama Love Spirit Chasing down a dream............................ 96

Reaching for the fruit... 98

Daddy Gentleness and Boy of Joy move the Earth.................. 100

The Gift of Heart (Sister Patience)............................. 102

Needle and Thread... 104

The Prayer of Passing On.. 105

Baby Kindness sleeping on a cloud 106

Baby Kindness takes baby steps.................................. 108

Brother Faith and Sister Patience on the phone................. 109

Boy of Joy protects the Earth................................... 110

Grandma Goodness goes to church................................. 112

Boy of Joy flies a kite... 114

Baby Kindness and Maya the Dog.................................. 116

Boy of Joy Holds the Earth on his back..........................118

The Spirit of Earth...121

Collection of Love in the Stationary mind......................123

Peace Love Karma

Our Motto-"To Create and Preserve Ecological and Spiritual Harmony on Earth"
Look for future books and products in the
"Spirit Comes to Earth" series by Eleven on our website
www.peacelovekarma.com

<u>Karma</u> is also known as
<u>The Law of Service:</u> Give and you shall receive
<u>The Law of Love:</u> You reap what you sow

About the Poet and Artist - Eleven

Eleven lives in lovely northern California with her daughter and Yorkshire terrier, Maya. She is seeking her purpose and spiritual gifts through art, song writing, poetry, engineering and parenting. She is the Creator, Poet and Artist of the "Spirit Comes to Earth" book series and cartoon characters. Visit Eleven's website at www.spiritcomestoearth.com

GIVE A GIFT FROM THE "SPIRIT COMES TO EARTH" BOOK SERIES TO YOUR FRIENDS OR FAMILY!

Check your local bookstore or Order through snail mail or website

- o   YES, I want ___ copies of "Spirit Comes to Earth - Renewing Your Heart's Mission (0-9743540-2-3) $19.95 for each case bound-hardcover book.
- o   WATCH FOR "Spirit Comes To Earth - Quit Eating your disease" and "Spirit Comes To Earth - Fearless Love" (Due out in 2005)

Please visit our website at **www.peacelovekarma.com** to place a paypal or credit card order or call our order line at **1-866-888-7272**. Or send check or money order for $19.95 plus $3.95 (Priority mail) or $1.95 (Media mail -4 weeks) shipping and handling per book and $1.95 for each additional book. Payment must accompany order. NO COD. CA. residents must pay state sales tax as applicable.(7.5%)
Provide your shipping address and check or money order payable to:
Peacelovekarma Publishing
c/o Art of Eleven - Book Orders
607 Elmira Rd. #266
Vacaville, CA. 95687

Name_____ _____
Organization_____
Address_____
City_____
State_____Zip code_____
Phone_____email_____

Please allow four to six weeks for delivery. Mail offer good for United States only. Copyright 2005 -Peace Love Karma Publishing

PRAISE FOR SPIRIT COMES TO EARTH:

"Eleven is a very gifted artist and writer. You are about to enter a world...full of God's love for people...full of love for one another and humanity. Read it. You will be touched like I was...forever."

Ron Dunivan - Country Music Artist/songwriter - Route 66 - CD across the World - www.dustbowlbaby.com